RITA JOE

Lnu and Indians We're Called

RAGWEED
THE ISLAND PUBLISHER

Artwork: Teresa MacPhee
Rock Drawings of the Micmac
The full image is reproduced on page 71.
Individual petroglyphs are duplicated for the cover
and the section title pages.

Editor: Lynn Henry
Cover & Book Design: Catherine Matthews
Printed & Bound in Canada by: Hignell Printing Ltd.

With thanks to The Canada Council for its generous support.

Ragweed Press
P.O. Box 2023
Charlottetown, Prince Edward Island
Canada C1A 7N7

Canadian Cataloguing in Publication Data
Joe, Rita, 1932–
    Lnu and Indians we're called
    ISBN 0-921556-22-5
1. Indians of North America — Poetry.
I. Title.

PS8569.0265L68 1991   C811'.54   C91-097652-X
PR9199.3.J63L68 1991

INTRODUCTION

◊

I try to have a positive outlook on life, and to reflect that in my writing. We all have hard times, but we cannot dwell on negative things. When I was one of the winners in the Literary Competition of the Nova Scotia Writers Federation, I remember thinking, "Now my people will think, if she can do it so can I." So, my context for writing is a positive one, and in my lectures at universities and schools I emphasize that point—no negativity. One way for native people to experience the positive parts of their culture is through spiritual productiveness. This is what I try to convey—there is a great need to tell our story in 1991, more than ever.

Rita Joe

CONTENTS

LNU AND INDIANS
WE'RE CALLED

I Clutch the Pretty Trinkets and the Pretty Beads

Many moons have passed since we stood on the shore
Waving to the people on ships going home.
Their gifts of pretty trinkets and pretty beads
I held close to my heart,
And their promises to return and to stay with us
Working side by side.
They returned and brought others, so many more,
Until we felt closed in, trying to learn their way
Adaptation became impossible.
They cleared much land, their buildings tall,
Monuments of their heroes standing in the midst
Of the stone wigwams that reach the sky.

I want to see the clouds but the stones are in my way
I want to walk the well-worn trails
But the stones hurt my moccasined feet.
I sweat in the close spaces, my brow misty with memories
The picture on my mind a wigwam
With laughing children, my language spoken by everyone
My clothes are heavy, so different
I want to cry but that is not our way.
The gifts of pretty trinkets
And the pretty beads I hold
The promise still beating the heart
Why do I feel so alone?
I clutch the pretty beads and the trinkets.

Lnu and Indians We're Called

In the year 1492
The man kept losing his way
By saving face to his queen
The lie he told lives today
The route he was longing to go
The riches of the land he must know
And the Nation he came on to see
Is the prize of the land and history

Chorus
For Lnu and Indians we're called
The Americas are known throughout the world
And all that is right and strong
Uniting the world we stand
For Lnu and Indians we're called
The power of the Nation the prize

In the year 1991
We are strangers and alone in the land
On saving face to our queen
We smile and sing the song
The loss of the man long ago
The riches of land you have known
And the Nation he came on to see
Is the prize of this land and history

Lnu—Indian

Atlantic Mission Conference, Burnt Church, N.B.

In the year 1492 Columbus sailed to America
The non-human he saw, his view wrong
We live to this day in the telling of books
That hang in the air

Then in 1510
Pope Julius II acknowledged us
A weary people with souls
Unforgotten in time
Travelling the lonely road of tears, ignoring future
Trying to recapture that which was lost

We live in spiritual harmony
Wisdom gained from the minds of old
Revived in trails left for the young.
The path is still in existence
We practise it with respect

In the mid-1600s were long robes
Showing the wrong we didn't know existed
The path is still there
Rekindling the fires of persuasion
Releasing the power.
These people of kindness, my people
Understanding the hidden trail, the *power*
The fancy still there in wonders of sincerity
Clinging to the old ways of truth and honesty

These are the people Columbus found
And each morning
Let them say the truth their way
Or nothing else

The Hidden Fence

Once upon a time I was in spaces free
I trod the lane of the rainbow road
My identity my own
And all the earth and sky my friend.
In barricaded fences of rescue
Submission becoming my prison
Now slowing to a trickle.
My stride becoming a shuffle
The feathers hanging limp as I signed the X

The spaces are still there for me to follow
In the wide open range
I teach you my culture
I want to teach you about me

Let me.

Analysis of my poem : 1

I

I am the Indian
And the burden lies yet with me

II

I see the spirit
The load on his back, heavy
He is unsure of himself, so very shy
The spring of the year awakens the song
He sings through his life, but
The pattern of history is in the way.
You ask why.

III

I see the spirit
The unloading is done through writing
Aboriginal across the land, tell our side
Tell it as it is, and gain pride
The spring of the year awakens your song,
The one I told.
Assumed fact is not always a true tale
In my role I'm recognized

Analysis of my poem : 2

I am the Indian
And the burden lies yet with me.

From the fountain the patterns fall
Cascading the being
Holding the soul
The seed alleviates and softens
Scaling the burden

How marvellous!
To deal with sight
To soar above the bounds
Of yesterday's fight.
The noble is precious now
How dear the culture.
I did not see the time that was
Or today,
But now I flow and murmur
Calling to attention

I Do Not Like Hearing the Wrong

I am all beaten inside
My country does not recognize me
The rest of the world acknowledges my person
Wishing my country would do the same
The Indian in me.

I tell the story the way it is,
The aboriginal part protesting
I tell the story with no holds barred
Because I do not like hearing the wrong
I am only reacting to an injustice
The dictation is too long coming.

The Aboriginal Greeting
For the Multi-Cultural Conference 1989

The offered hand is still in place
Extended to you since time began
And from where you came I honour your stay
My welcome,
From our sacred voice to your motherland.
The hand over one's heart I show you now
For multi-cultural we are in this country
I ask that you celebrate the native in me
To the many lands, from the places you have come.

YOU, I, LOVE,
BEAUTY, EARTH

You, I, Love, Beauty, Earth

Supposing you were I and I were you
You gave, I received

You would think in terms of love
Giving without thought of payment
The words of a culture
To spread and mend

Supposing I were you
And received without question
The words of a culture
Spreading news like yours

With so little, we share
But not so much of my life do you bear
Let us trade places just this once
And you listen while I go on about my culture
Important just like yours
But almost dead

Kujinaqq

I want to stand
Where our forefathers stood
To be as they were, from them came my roots

Simple learnings, without shame
Natural from expertise, my name

Sharings come unrestrained
The temptations of a hunt, curious
The high to the soul awakening

To stand again where my elders stood
The treasure of a legacy develops,
Admiration coming easily, because I understand

The grace of elegance blooming in mind
Trying to touch your heart, please listen!
I see the steady gain of man

Kujinaqq—Our Forefathers

Old Stories

There are stories told by the elderly
Of bannock baked in a bed of stone
Of birch bark fashioned into a pot
To boil meat and bone

There are tales told
Of what life was before
Of wigwam in the wood
With deerskin for a door

Fishing from canoe
Hunting in the wild
Herbs gathered for the sick
To cure and soothe

Prayers and song
Memories told to the young
When all life was Inua',kis

It will never be the same again
Only in our minds and elderly tales

Inua'kis—Indian

The Indian Blacksmith

Andrew Battiste of Eskasoni

Under the shade of leafy shelter
The Micmac swings the hammer
His brow shines with sweat
From the hot embers of his forge
The twang of the heavy beat, the sound of steel
The dying craft

Eel spears, drawknives, crooked knives
And lape'so'qn
The aboriginal cutter of basket strips

Throughout the years he worked
Singing songs to Niskam
Telling of traditions he knew
Now he is gone, his questions unanswered
"Why don't they understand my culture?
That I must cling to."

He shared his talent but others cannot see.

lape'so'qn—cutter of strips
Niskam—God

The Art of Making Quillboxes

In July, August, September and October
When it is the warmest part of summer
Maskwi' is ripe for stripping
To make quillboxes.

We look for the tree
The trunk the size of the bucket
The bark is good, we carve and cut
It peels away, coming to me

Now we look for quills
We see a porcupine
And throw a cloth on his back
Jumping behind, he aims the arrow
As if to say, "Leave me alone"
He waddles away

Now we have maskwi and kowi
To make quillboxes
The art of my people standing the ages
The skill like no other.

maskwi—birchbark
kowi—quills

Migration Indian

I toss and turn all through the night
The hurting bunk-boards, the hay and quilt not enough
The alarm rings, horizon turning red
We wash, dress, eat and take buckets
Rush to the fields of blue, like rivers out of sight.
And before noon we try to reach the quota
The songs in our head unsung
We work the blueberry fields
All muscle and might.

There is a way to hold rake, wrist in motion
Or to bend your back, legs wide, moving forward
Spacing your wind, going easy, your spirit cool
In spite of the sun on back, riding your shadow.
Then noontime, cold beans or bannock
Your thoughts speed back to the field
The song in your head inspiration
The blueberry fields we work
All muscle and might.

The long walk to the blower, to clean your berries
Waiting your turn, have a cigarette.
The comparing of notes and friendly chatter
Payday tonight, "Where's the best restaurant?"
Maybe phone home to Canada, bragging about quota
Then rest, not long, picking means money
The song in your head ready to sing
About the blueberry fields we work
All muscle and might.

We travel to find work, the migration Indian.

Free Trade

The Micmac Indian walked from the reservation to town
Where he knew there was water
In his pocket were only pennies
With five pennies he bought one herring for bait
And nearing the water, he bit the fish
Spitting the pieces into water
Creating the shimmering surface of oil
So the mackerel will come.
Then he fished to his heart's content.
Na'pola'ji' until there were many, so many indeed
He could hardly carry them

Then he went to the nearest town
Exchanging at each house for food or loose change

Then the long walk home to the reservation
With a coarse bag of food
And loose change, jingling in pocket.

Na'pola'ji'—putting fish on a forked stick

Indian Sketch

I saw beauty in the art
Someone drew
A pattern model she saw in our culture,
In a minority
The intensity was not broken
A warring pen sketched the wonder
Of a beaten race
The environmental movement cannot be curbed
Nor understood, unless you are Indian.

The picture will stay in everybody's mind
Providing our identity
Like the signature of a wigwam
Resting at the edge of the wood.

Sarah Denny

She is our culture
Knowing all
From birth to end
The christian song

She is a Micmac
Representing her call
Pounding her drum in song
And the art in telling is her draw

She is our culture
Knowing all
My friend Sarah
Relating our knowledge, we stand tall

Minuitaqn

I have named my craftshop Minuitaqn
Meaning "to re-create."
"To recreate what?" you say.
The crafts of my people, the Micmac
Inspiration swells in their heart
Ready to be fired by need
Then it flowers
There you see minuitaqn.
The creation is in their hands
It is native, and it is ours.

Minuitaqn—Recreate

Proposal for a Grant

I asked my superiors for a grant
To continue a business of arts and crafts
To create employment
And try to expand to a cultural centre,
A mini-museum and resources.
Busloads and busloads of children come to the house
Searching for knowledge of our culture.

I received a flat *No* with a lot of winding trails.
At the time I thought it was great for people to create
The happy eyes I saw when visitors handed me their craft.
Even teenagers producing for the first time,
Their work as beautiful as they were
Or the seniors reviving a hidden habit
Budding, just waiting to bloom.
I thought I was waving to sunshine
Trying to awaken the lost spirit
I am down but not done

You Are The Teacher

I wrote in verse what bothered me
The lies recorded in history
And beautiful words became my tool
Showing our life, a golden rule
And if our children today respond as much
You my people are their teacher,
Sharing,
They in turn will honour your word
And future generations they touch

A Special Friend

Ruth Holmes Whitehead

Somewhere there I have a friend
In this place without end
Written word we bring to view
Accumulating a purpose long overdue,
The message of unknown fame
For the native of our country
The Indian game.
Somewhere there I have a friend
The archives are her trade,
A chronicler bringing nobility
Together we relate the wonders of my nation,
Our song a landing place.

The Solid Part of One's Identity

In the expression of my tongue
I say, Kesalin? Do you love me?
I may say Kesalu'l, I love you.
Positive words are important
I do not teach hate
The solid part of one's identity
Is communication,
Exchanging words or touch
With no animosity towards another.
I have had positive experience
The past twenty-two years of writing
Trying to teach the Micmac way of life
The majority of the Micmacs are peace-keeping people
They are gentle people, anxious to please
I sympathize with my people across the nation
I admire what they think should be done
But do not think a militant attitude should be used
The solid part of our identity is sharing
That is why we are here today
We are survivors.

On Being Original

I like living close to nature
My ancestors did.
And being closer to the stars at night
And reading dreams
On interpretation, on what is right.

I like living close to nature
My parents did.
Meeting the sunrise at dawn
Upon seeing the sign of warmth
The sun song.

I like living close to nature:
I still do today.
Even improvising birch bark for a pot
To cook my meal.
The essence of my being original,
In my instincts.

Learning the Language

Look at the busy rivers
Where water runs over the pebbles
As if to say, "Hello, how are you? I am gone."
Or a leaf on a maple tree,
"Touch me but don't hurt."
You look but move on.

Lay on the grass
Mold your body to it, relaxing,
The spiritual in effect
And look at the sky,
The lazy roll of a cloud passing by
With pictures of dreams your mind wills
The reward of nature,
Gives you high high.

Kluskap O'kom

I left a message to Nikmaq
In the caves of stone
My home.
The message says I go away
But will return someday
And the sun will again shine
Across the trails my people walk.
Kluskap O'kom.

Kluskap O'Kom—Glooscap's home
Nikmaq—Micmac

◊

In Cape Breton, Nova Scotia there are caves at a place called Kelly's Mountain. The legend says that Klu'skap left and will return someday. The place is beautiful in the rising sun, hence the legend, passed from generation to generation. The multi-million dollar quarry nearby may destroy the caves. The inside of the cave has petroglyphs on the wall. These too will be destroyed.

◊ III

KESKMSI
(AHEAD OF MYSELF)

Unknown Regions

In early morning hours
I lay awake in wonder,
Trying to sort out my dreams
To determine their nature

They serve a rule of judgement
According to personal belief
They are there to bring messages
To tell partway of end

Environment
Giving guide to life
Like my people did long ago
True in spirit and childlike

The picture window sometimes happy
But worry plays a part
It depends on spirit of wonder
Determination winning the heart

That is why I like to read
The images playing the mind
In travel of unknown regions,
Revelation, a daring find

1937

The year 1937
My world comes tumbling down.
In childbirth my mother dies,
The baby goes with her.
"It was from the cold ice," they say,
Her fishing for smelts to feed the family.
Why her?
There were other people fishing.
Why her?
I shout even today.

I believe in fate, no alternative.
All the reasons we are who we are.
Me a foster child in so many homes
Being cared for by people as poor as I am.
We survive.

The year 1937
I saw moderation in bits or pieces.
The pictures like shadows, a veil at times
Like a puzzle, the pages turn slowly.
The scar is there like a bird of prey
Until it is written.

Don't turn the page, the hurt will be there again.
But I have to tell, this is life
I am gone, the word is all that is left.

The Road to Foster Home

Why is dad hanging onto a fencepost?
Why did grandmother fall down when the Chief spoke?
Why doesn't my sister Annabel answer my questions?

I am five years old
There are many things I do not understand
Like being taken to grandmother's house
Then back to our house
Where there is a lot of food on the table
I eat some cakes
Later I am carried by my father
To view mother in a long box

She is sleeping, they say
But she usually awakens when I call
She is so cold, "Cover her with a blanket, Dad."
He turns away, to face the wall

Finally they put the box in the ground
I hold somebody's hand

Grandma and Dad are hollering at each other
Dad wins the battle
We go away to some other place by train
It rocks back and forth, the wheels clatter

We arrive at the first foster home
If Dad can help it
There will be many more

The King and Queen Pass by on Train

I am happy
The King and Queen will pass by on train, they say
All the boys and girls on the reservation
Will receive pants, skirts and sailor blouses.
Our parcel arrives from the Indian Agency
To the foster home where I live
There is one sailor blouse, a skirt
My heart goes flip flop.
But the fun day goes by
With no one saying, "Put your blouse on."
My heart stops.

The day is over
Gone, my longing to see the King and the Queen.
And now my foster brother has new hand-made pants
With a sailor blouse to match.

My heart goes flip flop.

Keskmsi'

At age seven
I go to school
The teacher is talking
I do not understand much of what he says
So my stubby pencil makes contact
With a scrap of paper
I print small words,
The ones I know,
I try to put them in order.

"Bring that paper here," the teacher yells.
Timidly I walk, my knees trembling
I hand him the paper.
His eyes widen, "Where did you find these?"
I point at myself, my head, my heart,
The fear lessening.
He reads my first poem,
A jumble of words
Kes-km-si' na

I've caught up with myself,
That is why I am here
Poetry is my tool,
I create as I go
Kes-km-si' na, I tell you now.
Maybe tomorrow I will leave you,
Remember my stubby pencil,
and you too may "do."
Na kes-km-sit-isk naki'l elt.
You too will be ahead of yourself.

keskmsi'—ahead of myself

My Grandmother

A wrinkled face deep in thought.
Developed a respect
My awareness found.
In every line of her face
Expression revealed
The character of life.
The stolen fortune broke
In every line
There is a doorway to the soul
That shows the viewer,
And sadness unfolds.
In every line
The load is loosened
To shock the world
And sadden.
In every line
There are roadways of life
Giving testimony
To some forgotten plight.
In every line
Her age spoke truthfully,
Of rusty chains of existence
Of yesterday's fight.

How dear she looks
She is my grandmother
A picture in an old album.

The Monk

I am tired in early evening
I lay on the couch relaxing in a half-doze.
This is the seventh month of pregnancy.
A spirit-monk is bending over my stomach
Looking, as if with concern;
I wish him away.
A short time later I go to hospital
Today I have a strapping boy
That a monk came to see one day.

The Toddler Boy From Another Age

After the birth of my baby
I slept on a cot near the infant
In the old dining room
Of a house we had purchased.
During the night my newborn cried a need.
Instantly I swung my feet onto the floor
Eager to comfort my offspring.
A little toddler ran across my path
On his way back I reached out my hand
To hug and keep him warm.
The stretch of hand produced air
And he ran away to hide behind a crib.
Like all little boys in mischief his eyes dared
But with no fear from him or me
Both of us seemed to care.

Once in a while he comes to his former home
The toddler boy from another age
Now a shadow.

Reunion

After having not seen each other for twenty years
My brother Roddy and I met in Maine.

I saw him standing there
His dark hair tied back with a kerchief
He looked Indian, so dear
I ran across the parking lot and hugged him
The people who saw us knew our story
Their eyes filled with tears
The long separation, while I looked after my family
He lived so far away
Until that day we met in Maine, U.S.A.

The Dream Was The Answer

On the morning of August 14, 1989
My husband Frank passed away in Calais, Maine.
The thirty-five years we spent together
Is a love story in itself, always there.
I respected the man and lost him
Ki'su'lk weswalata.

The next morning on the way home to Canada
We rested in New Brunswick.
My grandson the driver sleeping
While my thoughts kept me awake
The pain so great, I conversed with Niskam
I tried to convice him that Frank was a good man
He knew a lot of trades I told him,
One of them with children.
As a worker for the Micmac Family and Children Services
He replaced loss with loving arms.

On the morning of September 14, 1989
I received a phone call from Saskatchewan
Where our daughter Bernadette trains
To better herself, more determined now
That her father is gone.
"I dreamt about Dad," she said
"He was holding a child, a child so beautiful
His hair the colour of snow."
I knew then that Frank is at peace
The symbol of our culture is white
He is working with Niskam now I know.

> *Ki'su'lk weswalata'*—*Our Creator took him*
> *Niskam*—*God*

The Man In An Indian Jacket

In my bed one night I awoke to a sensation of touch
A man was peering down at me
As if with concern.
A beautiful jacket hung on his lean frame
The fringes swinging with every move
His stride the sureness of man.
The face I could not see, it was circled in fog
Then he turned, going through the wall.
I jumped out of bed in search of him
And seeing the secure door, knew he was supernatural.
I returned to my bed, placing a child on either side of me
Acting on what mother taught,
The innocence of children.
Reciting the Lord's prayer,
My gaze holding the symbol on the wall,
Soon I slept.

The next day I told my mother
"The in-laws" she said. "Ask them."
Sure enough, they had a relative
Who had a favourite jacket.
The late Grand Chief John Denny
My in-law kin from another age.

◊   Grand Chief John Denny died in 1919.

The Great Brave

Oh Niskam the Great Brave
Touch the feathers of my bonnet
So that my spirit may rise
Not anxious as I was before
Lay your hand upon my brow
My shadow
In tune to your goodness I bow
Touch the leather I wear with humility
Touch it gently like the soft breeze
A gentle sigh
I love you my Great Brave
I love the wind whisper through the trees
The four seasons play and are gone
The spiritual phenomena of early dawn
The gift of knowledge in so many ways
The woven eloquence you helped me raise
Touch my moccasins and the beads
That we may always represent you in peace
Touch them gently
They are the representation of my dreams
I love you my Great Brave
I thank you.

Niskam—God

St. Ann's Picture On Deerhide

Her painted image hangs on my wall
On tanned skin with ragged fringe
Her kind eyes and gentle mouth
Remind me of a grandmother
Who may intercede for me when trouble arises

Her likeness was put into our care long ago
By long robes. Their teaching told
That she is the grandmother of Niskam
The Kji-Saqamow in the sky.
We then told our children, the many generations,
With the oral weight we always carry.
The beautiful St. Ann we love
Our kijinu' in the sky.

Niskam—God
Kji-Saqamow—Great Chief
kijinu'—grandmother

He Is There At the Edge of The Woods

I see the baby Niskam
When the white snow is on the ground
The branches hanging down with their load
All still, with no sound

I see him there at the edge of the woods
To my eyes like a feathered brave
The essence of all of my life
Showing beauty to all the world

I see him there at the edge of the woods
Reminding me that he is my Kji-Saqmaw
Reality is the cap in my hand
And humility plays the most part

I see him there at the edge of the woods
When the white snow is on the ground
He is our babe as surely as he is native,
For all cultures he is their own

Niskam—God
Kji-Saqmaw—Grand Chief

Wikwom Church in Millbrook N.S.

A wave of warmth cradled my soul
When I saw the wikwom church on Millbrook reserve
I saw the basket-woven patkwialasutmaqn
Gratitude came
When I saw the Micmac-written stations of the cross

I perceived an offering of a symbol
To magnify my belief
The heart and mind declaring the truth
We rely on so much

The warmth will stay in my shadow
Because my cultural brand marks my trail
To my Niskam

wikwom—wigwam
patkwialsutmaqn—altar
Niskam—God

Malikewe'j

In the wooded area of the balsam trees
We were sitting on the welcome earth
We heard the gentle waves on shore
And the lullaby of birds, our bond
The scenes that never fade
Near the grotto church of Malikewe'j.

We see Niskam as great
Our ancestors are home with him
And we know
That if childlike rewards are totalled same
My grandsire leads the way
These are the scenes that never fade
Near the grotto church of Malikewe'j.

We are part of the blessed earth
The balsam is always near
The spirits there,
We are them
Unforgettable is love,
The link remains
These are the scenes which never fade
Near the grotto church of Malikewe'j.

Malikewe'j—Malagawatch, Cape Breton, N.S.
Niskam—God

Chapel Island Today

At first of time
My wigwam stood beneath the sky
The animals, birds and the earth my friend
The life spare, until we were many, so many
My kin said, "As much as the hairs on my head."

Then long robes came
Enlightening on gift that which was mine,
Our spirituality held, even on forbidden ground
The treasure they learn today
Proclaiming on wisdom my people held.

Today, wigwams are of different kind
Of clapboard, plywood, canvas
But still there beneath the sky.
And reality awakens each new day
Our Chapel Island the ongoing history
Where all our dreams of happiness lay.

THE WISHING GAME

Prejudice Is Something We Can Do Without

I walk into a store in town
My pockets bursting with money
My needs are like any other
For goods I want to buy in a hurry
The clerk in the store sees my face, the rugged clothes
My feet in mukluks, the headband on my brow

She has immediate ideas of the poor Indian,
The stereotype in progress
She does not know I sense ill will
So gently I turn around and walk out,
Looking for another store

One where the clerk is all smiles, even if it hurts
I have bought out the store,
My pockets empty
Prejudice is something we can do without
Accept me just as I am,
My money, and my identity

The Story Needs To Be Told

My moccasin trod on lonely trails,
I needed to learn about life
Where my country failed.
I made them see I never died
My emblems withstood the flood
The twisted tried.
How do I tell them?
I'm only human
The message of time declaring a stay
From the strong and stubborn shadow.

My story needs to be told
In the learning halls of our country's great
Then, and only then
You will see me as I am
My heart in the extended hand
Offered in friendship

Please tell them.

Justice

Justice seems to have many faces
It does not want to play if my skin is not the right hue,
Or correct the wrong we long for,
Action hanging off-balance
Justice is like an open field
We observe, but are afraid to approach.
We have been burned before
Hence the broken stride
And the lingering doubt
We often hide

Justice may want to play
If we have an open smile
And offer the hand of communication
To make it worthwhile

Justice has to make me see
Hear, feel.
Then I will know the truth is like a toy
To be enjoyed or broken

Battered Women

The battered women in all walks of life are there
The ill-treatment we undergo, psyches us out
Jumping to do our duties, reasoning love
Obeying blindly, until it is too much to bear.
At first I hid my hurt in long-sleeve blouses
The ache in my heart driving lonely thoughts inward
Believing the love-words, dependent
Our children there looking up to me
Wanting to believe so very much, the love reward.
This went on for years at first.
Most of the time we were compatible, friendly
But liquor always got its way.
After a while I began to search for safety,
In the mind as well as the physical,
With other people
Sharing my story with anyone listening
Especially with other women, searching for outlets
Emphasizing how much love was there
But liquor and mistreatment going together.
Our togetherness unsettled, I began to write
He made fun, but I built my spirit, using culture.
Today I share my story with you
The building comes down sometimes
But we women, by association,
Always stand together.

My Crutch

In the quiet loss of dignity
I run to escape my problem
The alcoholic load I use as a crutch,
My body numb
And the loud noise I hear in the mind
My insides bind
My life a mess, moving onward blind

I need a foundation like long ago
Where everything depended on survival
And our nation grew
Love and strength multiplied the gifts
To my person now due

I wish the tail were without blockades
Then I would walk with ease
My life there is an open book
My country, please
The inner drive is always there
Wanting to give pleasure
But the crutch is easy to hold,
The wrong pictured
There is good, there is good
The Indian of 1991

Indian Residential Schools

Today on television I heard a discussion
Of residential schools across the country.
I saw a man talk about sex abuse done to him
He even had a hard time saying it.
I was in one of the schools, my daughter too
There was physical abuse where I was
Not sex but mind mistreatment.
To me there was one individual who did this
As always there are certain people who do.
The rest of the nuns were tolerable
The priest in my time a kind man.

My daughter says she didn't have it hard
But again only one person did her wrong
And upon seeing her in later years
This person hugged her and cried
My daughter knew the forgiving song.

I know for a fact people who came from schools
Have turned into productive persons.
Even women who had it hard have become nuns
And men from across the country their dreams realized.
In my case I've nobody to blame for being there
I put myself where I would receive training
The four years have given me strength
My life to this day has gained courage
I know who I am, and my people are the prize.

Demasduit

On March 1819, the Beothuks were surprised and killed.
Demasduit survived.
She just had given birth to a babe
All mothers on earth consider a prize.
A man, her captor, the all-powerful white
Committed a crime
Nobody paid.
Chief Nonosbawsut, her husband, tried with his life
But nobody paid.
I implore for Demasduit,
Mary March they named her,
I implore, know her,
But not her killer.
Know Demasduit
The last of the Beothuks of Ktaqmkuk

Ktaqmkuk—Newfoundland

I'm A Beothuk

"I'm a Beothuk," my son announced
"They didn't all die like history says."

My husband Frank Joe, his roots were from Ktaqmkuk
His father Stephen Joe came across looking for a wife
And he married a Micmac from Po'tlo'tek
Producing two girls and two boys,
One of them my husband.

Today my children dream of their ancestry
Being Beothuk, the grain flowing in them
I let them dream, even encouraging a possibility
Because I wonder, perhaps they were not all erased
And that speck of sand flows in my children.

Ktaqmkuk—Newfoundland
Po'tlo'tek—Chapel Island

The Ksan Dancers of British Columbia

In capes of dark
With colourful designs
They dance the legends of yesterday

With dances of joy
And imitations of animal kingdoms
They act the songs of yesterday

In leather cloth
The buckskin of reminisence
They dance the monuments of yesterday

How true they dance
Instilling pride for tomorrow
The sketches land upon the heart to all tribes
We relate with them
The Ksan dancers of British Columbia.

A Pow-wow in Shubenacadie

I enter the multi-purpose building
Where the pow-wow is held
And stand amidst the crowd
Hoping to see someone familiar, to say hello
The drummers begin to play, singing songs
That touch my heart
A man comes out of the crowd,
and dances by me.
I am curious, "Who is he?" I ask.
A medicine man from out of the province, I am told.
I join the dance, sometimes closing my eyes,
Dancing the elderly woman dance,
My feet flat, close to earth
The song takes a long time to end
And we dance
When I walk away from the floor
My feet are light, I walk on air
and I feel fear.
I explain the feeling to a medicine man.
"You have been in a ceremonial healing dance,"
he says, "Sit out the next one."
So I sit, amazement in my heart,
ready to tell about the elderly woman dance.

Oka

My good people in Oka
My heart goes to you
The sadness weighing on my soul like a heavy stone.
I see your faces and bodies in the crowd
Stormy, agitated,
Our children looking on, confused, uncertain.
I know you are angry, I am the same
I know the hurt in progress since discovery.
But my spirit is vague, wanting to help
Anger not dwelling
I want to help in another way, into the future.
To earn my way into the uncultured blockade
The stone-throwing without thought
Knowledge in limbo.
They are only few,
The majority wanting to help.
Let them do their thing my good people in Oka
I know it will be slow,.
But it will be done.
I now the cultured spirits in our country
Move like the wind, unseen but felt
A gentle caress moving mountains, into another century.
Yes, my good people of Oka
We will complete the circle, we will dry our tears
Because we are survivors, the identity of Canada
We are the country's symbol
Peace!

Oka Song

The native of the land is still a stranger
The native of the land is in no man's land
The fences of our feeling for the stranger
We tend to hold and not understand.
The soldier guns don't look good today
Our country does not understand the way.
How do we mend the sadness?
Listen just this time and pretend you care.

Chorus
Why don't you try to take the hurt away
Why don't you take my hand and say
I was so wrong to cause pain that way
And Oka came as we tried to stop war that day.

Though my heart beats like a drum today
And my heart is in my thoughts to vow
I will pave the way to make amends and say,
We started out wrong, just be friends for now.
And the children's spirits must bend
When they see our shining eyes
The sadness of the eyes, we cannot hide
They show the world the hurt inside.

Dancing Eagle

Today I am at a pow-wow
It is a gathering of native people
We dance, sing, play drums, dress traditional
Nobody is shy, we are all Indian
Today I practice my tradition free.
Today I am in the lead at the Grand Entrance
The dance that is done for the opening ceremonies.

There is a great feast
All traditional food is served
Everybody is a friend, they shake my hand
Because I am from a different area of Canada.

In the early morning hour
Many of us do a sweat in the sweatlodge
My Kisu'lk is on my mind while doing the sweat.
Many hours later we finish, I am tired
Somebody tells me to lay down and sleep under a tree
I lay down with no care in the world, soon asleep.
One hour later I awaken and look at the sky
I see a man dancing with a mandella in his hand
And an honour stick in the other.
He is in full regalia
Dancing, dancing.
I lift my arms to the sky giving thanks
I have had a vision
I have seen something very few people see
I have seen the Dancing Eagle
My Kisu'lk in the sky.

Kisu'lk—Creator

The Order of Canada

The bus arrives at Rideau Hall
The home of the Governor General of Canada.
The place seemed the most inaccessible of all
But here I am on April 18, 1990
To receive an award.
The recipients are led to their seats
An aide gives direction about protocol
All around we are polite with one another
Everybody with their own thoughts.
From the last row the names in sequence are called
Finally the man next to me is receiving
I start to shiver, my hands sweat.
I know I'm going to stumble thinking to myself.
"Niskam apoqnmui'."

"Frank are you there? I'm happy! Are you? I am."
These are the things we used to say to each other
It seems such a short time ago.
Rita Joe, I hear the name
I do not remember rising, a floating sensation
Until I stand before the Governor General of Canada.
He pins the medal, "The Order of Canada,"
I look into his eyes, they are kind.
"Thank you," I murmur.
I sign the register
And staring into the people's eyes, searching for wonder
They shine, receiving my answer
To me the medal is for my people, the coming generation
The greeting of the hand over the heart has earned a merit
Thank you my country for accepting my salutation.

Niskam apoqnmui'—God help me

The Wishing Game

I travel over land and sea
Urging you to see our way of peace
Forgotten there my ways became
Remember them,
They are passing fame.
I must tell, my people say
Together we must find a middle way
Come and see how we live today
Only then will you know my nation well.

Chorus
Together we find the wishing game
That all the people know each other well
Together we find the wishing game
That in this country we live in peaceful way

Na milteskm na maqmikew
Welakumki'k welek na nemitu'
Awanta'si'k na telo'lti'k
Nenwite'ten ke'luk wejitu'k
Telimki'k mta elu'li'oqq
Toqi'weji'tuk na mawiomi
Jukita'q na jikeywinen
Kisi'kjiji'wi'tesnen na tujiw

Toqi'kwilmne'j na weloti'
Na msit welikjiji'tultisnu' etuk
Toqi'kwilmne'j na weloti'
Na tan wiki'k wela'matultisnu'.

Tomorrow's Blessing

"If I were you" folks often say
"I would go to college to learn about people."
Then I would answer
I have discovered good things already
My people's lives unchanged, the spiritual flame aglow
The sharing thoughts, the prize in expectation
For tomorrow's blessing.

I do not even try to consider
The assumed fact, often misleading
My guidance is being with them
Learning firsthand
To observe and record
Fostering the belief in declaration
My theatre on the reservation, the front row
What else does one need?
But by telling the love
I have always known
The seed, someday fullblown.

I Am An Indian On This Land

I am just an Indian on this land
I am sad, my culture you do not understand.
I am just an Indian to you now
You wrinkle your brow

Today you greet me with bagpipes
Today you sing your songs to me
Today we shake hands and see
How we keep good company.
Today I will tell stories
Today I play the drum and dance
Today I will say what is on my mind
For being friends is our goal.
Today I will show I am just like you
Today I will show what is true
Today I will show we can be friends
Together we agree.
Today I will tell about my race
Today I will share what is mine
Today I give you my heart
This is all we own.
Today I show.
Hello everybody, my name is Rita Joe.

ROCK DRAWINGS OF THE MICMAC

The rock drawings (petroglyphs) which border the central image are borrowed from the McGowen Lake, Fairy Bay sites of Kejimikujik Park in Nova Scotia. Ethnologists and Micmac sources believe that the images describe religious journeys, commemorate celebrations and puberty rituals, and depict animal spirits common to Micmac lore.

The central image is the eight-pointed star. This motif has been employed by the Micmac for centuries in ancient legends and continues to symbolize unity today. The eight arms of the star point in the four cardinal directions. The number four speaks of balance in the four directions and within the person—the number four is doubled to reflect understanding that all that one sees is not necessarily all that is perceptible (The Great Mystery).

In oral tradition, the Micmac, like all other people, originated from the centre of the earth. Four groups of people were created: the red, the yellow, the black and the white. These colours are also the primary colours associated with the four directions. Each group was sent to one of the four directions with a mission to carry out. When the mission was completed, the groups were to return to the centre, where there would be great harmony. The circle surrounding the eight-pointed star is an acknowledgement of the sun that surrounds the people of all clans.

The sun/eight-pointed star can be further interpreted as a compass. The lines on the star that point north align to true north and, on summer solstice, to magnetic north. The sun, giver of life, is central to fertility rituals. The triangular figure to the left is a geometric ideogram for woman—giver of life. The triangle represents life-giving energy. Women were the primary makers of rock drawings, and the only makers of female images.

The site of the petroglyphs is as significant to the Micmac tradition as the drawings themselves. The area now called Bedford, from where the central image is derived, has been a gathering place for the Micmac since time immemorial. The Bedford Barrens rise up out of the Basin like whale-backs on the sea—in keeping with Micmac belief that all things of the land are alive, the area is referred to as the place of the whale-backs. Moving eastward and away from the carvings is a large amphitheatre. At its centre rests a feldspar stone that is not common to the area, and in the stone's centre is a carved circle. A circle of birches to the right of the stone marks a deposit of upright stones. These circles are all dependant on one another — they acknowledge unseen powers, the life-giving forces represented by the circle, the heart of the Micmac belief system.

Teresa MacPhee